# A Nod to God
## *His Lighter Side in Verse*

Carolyn Burkholder

REVISED EDITION

Corra Harris Chapel Window
Cherokee County, Georgia

# *Endorsements*

Ms. Burkholder has cleverly put to poetic verse stories of the lively characters of the Bible. The reader will delight in viewing with "new eyes" the exploits, flaws, and foibles of these beloved and VERY human instruments of God's purposes. Enjoy!
—Rev. DeDe W. Leetch, Ordained Elder, retired, Former District Superintendent, North Georgia Conference, United Methodist Church

Carolyn Burkholder has put together an unusual and creative presentation of Biblical personalities that is entertaining and insightful.
—Bill Crews, Author of *Bones on the Chisholm Trail, Bones Indiana Country, Prairie Sunshine,* and *Bones on the Severs Ranch: An Oklahoma Thriller*

If God has a sense of humor, as I have always believed, then He must be smiling at Carolyn Burkholder's collection of light verse based on her favorite biblical passages. The multi-talented Mrs. Burkholder has shown that religion need not be the somber affair that conventional wisdom has often held. As the scripture says, "Make a joyful noise unto the Lord." Her poems are just that: a joyful noise.
—Richard Dowis, Author of *The Tender Leaves of Hope*

# A Nod to God
## His Lighter Side in Verse

### Carolyn Burkholder

### Illustrations by Jim Bennett

Carolyn's Creations
Waleska, Georgia

Copyright © 2013 Carolyn Burkholder
All rights reserved.

ISBN: 0988272415
ISBN 13: 9780988272415
Library of Congress Control Number: 2012922387
Carolyn's Creations Waleska, GA

*For my husband, Dan,
who tirelessly and patiently
listened to every poem,
soothed my frazzled nerves,
and solved my computer glitches.*

*Be glad in the Lord, and rejoice ye righteous:*
*And shout for joy, all ye that are upright in the Lord.*
*Psalms 32:11*

# Contents

A Word from the Author · · · · · · · · · · · · · · · · · · · · · · · · · · · · · 1
Majestic Oak at Sunrise · · · · · · · · · · · · · · · · · · · · · · · · · · · · · 2
God, the Almighty · · · · · · · · · · · · · · · · · · · · · · · · · · · · · · · · · 3
Adam and Eve · · · · · · · · · · · · · · · · · · · · · · · · · · · · · · · · · · · · 7
Noah · · · · · · · · · · · · · · · · · · · · · · · · · · · · · · · · · · · · · · · · · · 11
Noah and His Funny Boat · · · · · · · · · · · · · · · · · · · · · · · · · · · · 13
Llama With Beautiful Eyes · · · · · · · · · · · · · · · · · · · · · · · · · · · 16
Jacob and Esau · · · · · · · · · · · · · · · · · · · · · · · · · · · · · · · · · · · 17
Jacob--The Grabber · · · · · · · · · · · · · · · · · · · · · · · · · · · · · · · · 21
Storm Clouds · · · · · · · · · · · · · · · · · · · · · · · · · · · · · · · · · · · · 26
Job · · · · · · · · · · · · · · · · · · · · · · · · · · · · · · · · · · · · · · · · · · · · 27
Rahab · · · · · · · · · · · · · · · · · · · · · · · · · · · · · · · · · · · · · · · · · · 33
David · · · · · · · · · · · · · · · · · · · · · · · · · · · · · · · · · · · · · · · · · · 37
Sheaf of Wheat · · · · · · · · · · · · · · · · · · · · · · · · · · · · · · · · · · · 42
Solomon · · · · · · · · · · · · · · · · · · · · · · · · · · · · · · · · · · · · · · · · 43
Elijah · · · · · · · · · · · · · · · · · · · · · · · · · · · · · · · · · · · · · · · · · · 49
Elijah Was a Prophet, Yeah! · · · · · · · · · · · · · · · · · · · · · · · · · 51
Titmouse and Angel · · · · · · · · · · · · · · · · · · · · · · · · · · · · · · · 54
Jeremiah-The Weeping Prophet · · · · · · · · · · · · · · · · · · · · · · 55
Roman Coliseum · · · · · · · · · · · · · · · · · · · · · · · · · · · · · · · · · 58
Daniel · · · · · · · · · · · · · · · · · · · · · · · · · · · · · · · · · · · · · · · · · · 59
Ezekiel · · · · · · · · · · · · · · · · · · · · · · · · · · · · · · · · · · · · · · · · · 65
Columns · · · · · · · · · · · · · · · · · · · · · · · · · · · · · · · · · · · · · · · 70
Haggai · · · · · · · · · · · · · · · · · · · · · · · · · · · · · · · · · · · · · · · · · 71
Esther · · · · · · · · · · · · · · · · · · · · · · · · · · · · · · · · · · · · · · · · · 75
Esther--For Such A Time As This · · · · · · · · · · · · · · · · · · · · · 77
The Written Word · · · · · · · · · · · · · · · · · · · · · · · · · · · · · · · · 82

| | |
|---|---|
| Ezra | 83 |
| Communion Cup | 86 |
| Nehemiah | 87 |
| Angel Lights | 90 |
| Gabriel | 91 |
| Zechariah | 95 |
| Madonna and Child | 100 |
| Mary, Mother of Jesus | 101 |
| Mary, the Teen | 102 |
| Sister Angels Tree Carving | 106 |
| Elizabeth | 107 |
| Elizabeth and Mary | 109 |
| Dove at the Hermitage | 112 |
| Simeon and Anna | 113 |
| Peter | 118 |
| Simon Peter | 119 |
| Olive Tree | 124 |
| Zacchaeus | 125 |
| Zacchaeus, the Little Man | 127 |
| Mary and Martha | 131 |
| Portrait of a Tree | 136 |
| Judas Iscariot | 137 |
| Judas Iscariot–Quite a Study | 139 |
| Tree at Manassas Battlefield | 142 |
| Barabbas | 143 |
| Twin Roads | 146 |
| Paul, Da' Man | 147 |
| Carving on Door | 152 |
| Jesus | 153 |
| Acknowledgements | 157 |
| Illustrations and Photographs | 159 |

# *A Word from the Author*

Sir William Osler said, "Laughter is the music of life." I truly believe that. What do we do when we are happy or joyful? We grin; we smile; we laugh. Sometimes, it just bubbles out of us, and there is nothing we can do to control it. And how do we feel after that good, hard belly laugh? Relaxed, content, even happier. Laughter is healing; it gives relief from stress, sadness, or anger.

Laughter is truly a gift from God. After all, we are made in His image, so God must also have a sense of humor. Just look at all the funny things and creatures in this world, some truly hilarious. As Karl Barth said, "Laughter is the closest thing to the grace of God."

When I began to explore the Bible and the characters in it, I found that the Holy Bible is permeated with humor. Once I began to see the characters and situations from a very human frame of reference and began to read the Bible, looking for the humor, I found it everywhere and in many different forms.

Using several different versions of the Bible, I began to write humorous poems about some of the characters. The poems are not only light-hearted, but they tell stories about the Biblical characters' spiritual faith. Hopefully, they make each character come alive, become real and very human. I have loved writing the poems and hope that you will also enjoy them.

If they inspire you to laugh more and read further in the Bible as you look for other illustrations of God's humor, then I will have accomplished my goal.

Majestic Oak at Sunrise
Waleska, Georgia

## *God, the Almighty*

Yes, God created
The heavens and earth.
To every thing
He gave it birth.

He was sitting around
Bored one day
With nothing to do
In the void, let's say.

He was tired of playing
Solitaire alone
As He sat by Himself
On that great big throne,

So He thought and thought
And decided to add
A few things around Him.
He got out His pad.

Let's see, what to do first?
Yes, I'll start with light.
It's hard to see
So we need day and night.

Yes, God
Let His imagination go free!
As He created the sky,
The land, and the sea.

He was on a roll
And having a ball.
He put in the sun and moon
Tight, not to fall.

He really went wild
Putting creatures together.
He made them unique:
Either fur, fin, or feather.

He thought He was done
And decided to rest,
But what was missing
Was surely the best.

Yes, God decided
He wanted a friend,
So He created humans.
And that was the end.

He had something to do,
No doubt about that.
We've kept Him quite busy
As we bred and begat.

Now He's always busy
With us every day.
Too bad, 'cause now He has
No time to play!

## Adam and Eve

## *Adam and Eve*

## *Genesis 4, 5*

God fashioned Adam from the dust of the ground and gave him life by blowing into his nostrils. Adam was in charge of the Garden of Eden and all the animals, but Adam was still lonely, so God created woman--Eve-- from one of Adam's ribs.

Adam and Eve lived in this Paradise and could eat anything they wanted except from the Tree of the Knowledge of Good and Evil.

One day, a serpent entered and tempted Eve to eat of the Tree. She ate the fruit and gave some to Adam, who also ate it. Then they both became aware that they were naked and tried to hide from God. Of course, God knew their sin and expelled them forever from His garden.

## *Adam & Eve*

God was so pleased with all that He'd made
He decided to share it with a man and a maid,
So He gathered the dust and rolled it around
And made man alive from the dirt of the ground.

Poor Adam was lonely and craved a mate.
He wanted a woman; he wanted a date.
So out of Adam, God took a rib
And that was the beginning of women's lib.

The Garden of Eden was their new home.
It was quite a sight; they were free to roam.
All that was there they were free to eat,
Except of one tree, which could be a treat.

The Serpent slid in and made his pitch.
He said God was wrong and made Eve itch
To be like God and know good from evil,
And that was what started the whole upheaval.

It was so good she called Adam to share,
And listening to her would be his burden to bear.
Their eyes were opened to their naked state,
And they hid from God, awaiting their fate.

God was upset and He wanted to know why
They knew they were naked, exposed to the eye.
"It was Eve," said Adam. "It was the serpent," said Eve.
But God knew the truth and said, " You must leave.

"You no longer can live in Paradise—
You will labor and sweat and pay a great price.
You will be scattered upon the earth,
And in great pain, your children you'll birth."

So Adam and Eve left the perfect garden.
They would ever seek to achieve God's pardon.

# *Noah*

## *c. 2300 B.C.*

## *Genesis 5:29*

Noah was 600 years old at the time of the Bible story and a very righteous man. He was the ninth generation of Adam and Eve and was the grandson of Methuselah. At that time, all the world seemed to be corrupt, and God decided just to get rid of everyone and start over. He chose Noah to be saved and to perpetuate the human race, so our entire human race has descended from Noah's three sons after the flood.

God decided to use floodwaters to destroy everything. He warned Noah of the impending flood and made a covenant with him to save Noah and his family. Noah was instructed to build an ark and was given the exact dimensions. God also told him to take with him on the ark a male and a female of every animal, reptile, and bird on the earth, so they could replenish it after the flood.

Noah did exactly as he was told, and on the appointed week, he and all his family boarded the boat along with 45,000 animals.

Finally, the rains came for forty days and nights and covered even the tallest mountain. We don't know how long they were all on the boat, but Noah aged from 600 to 700 years old during that time. God made a pact never again to curse the earth on humankind's account.

## *Noah and His Funny Boat*

What must the neighbors have thought
When Noah started in on his boat?
The land was dry, no sign of rain.
No reason to go afloat.

I'll bet they laughed and scoffed
As Noah set about his job,
For God had selected Noah,
Picked him out from the mob.

He was the only faithful one,
True to God's every word.
All others had become corrupt—
The violence was absurd.

So God decided to end it all,
Sorry he had created this mess,
But still decided to save our man
And all his family - *yes!*

Now Noah was no longer young.
Even then, 600 was old.
But he got to work a-buildin',
Just as he was told.

The ark was huge—imagine it.
As tall as a redwood tree,
Longer than a football field,
And seaworthy, believe you me.

The ark was done and ready to go.
Animals came from far and wide.
Two by two, they entered the boat
To be safe from the flood outside.

It took a week to get them all in
And in their rightful places.
It must have been hard to separate
And to juggle all the races.

How would He keep the monkeys calm
And the lions from having a feast,
And what in the world would he do
If all the young rabbits increased?

Woodpeckers might make holes
In the side of the wooden ark!
And how about the termites?
Noah had no walk in the park.

For forty days and forty nights
The rain came down without stopping
Until the ark floated above it all,
Thoroughly wet and sopping.

At last, the rain quit as God said it would,
And Noah sent out the birds
To check for dry land and get rid of
The resident flocks and herds.

Wow! What patience this man had
Not only to build his boat,
But then to be so confined
With his kids and a Billy Goat.

**Llama With Beautiful Eyes**
**Waleska, Georgia**

# *Jacob and Esau*

## *c. 2006 B.C.*

## *Genesis 25-50*

There were four stages in Jacob's life, each marking a personal experience with God. Jacob was born to Isaac and Rebekah, and had a twin brother, Esau, who actually was born first. Jacob grabbed onto Esau's heel as they were being born. They were very different. Esau became a hunter and was Isaac's favorite, while Jacob was a quieter person, a farmer, and was Rebekah's favorite.

Esau traded his birthright to Jacob for a bowl of stew. Later, when Isaac was blind and ill, he decided to bestow his blessing of the firstborn upon Esau. Jacob pretended to be Esau and deceitfully grabbed the blessing rightfully belonging to Esau, who was then reduced to serving his brother. Esau vowed to kill him, so Jacob went to live with relatives. On the way there, he had a vision of a ladder reaching to heaven with angels going up and down, and he heard the sound of God's voice giving him more blessings--stage two.

In stage three, Jacob met Rachel and worked seven years to gain her hand only to be deceived into marrying her older sister, Leah, so he worked another seven years to finally gain Rachel's hand in marriage. Jacob returned to Canaan with his family and servants. Again, on the way, he encountered a heavenly being. They wrestled all night, and Jacob would not let him go until the Being blessed him.

In the last stage, God grabbed onto Jacob so tightly that Jacob was unwilling to make a move without God's approval. Jacob became the father of the twelve tribes of Israel.

## *Jacob and Esau*

The story of Jacob and Esau
Is a very sad story indeed.
Esau was born first,
Full of jealousy and greed.

He was Isaac's favorite;
He liked Esau the best.
While Rebekah favored Jacob,
And it became a contest.

Esau was a hunter
Who pursued the wild game,
While Jacob was a farmer.
He was quieter and tame.

Esau was the oldest,
Setting Jacob to obsessing,
Until he tricked his dad
And got the firstborn blessing.

Not only that,
But Jacob wanted it all.
He schemed, got Esau's birthright,
Not subject to recall.

Esau would be second forever;
He soon realized his fate.
He threatened to kill Jacob.
He wanted to set things straight.

But Jacob got wind of the plan,
And he decided to split,
Even though he was guilty,
He had to readily admit.

So, brother against brother,
The theme rose up again.
It is very sad, but true—
The age-old story of man.

## *Jacob--The Grabber*

Jacob was determined
From the very start
To take what he could get,
And not just his own part.

At birth, he grabbed a hold
Onto his brother's heel.
Esau's being first,
For Jake, was a raw deal.

A hairy dude was Esau,
A real good hunter he.
He took his birthright lightly;
Turned out, t'was a pity....

Jacob was quite different,
Not Esau-esque at all.
Serious and quiet,
Next to Esau, he was small.

Esau was a carefree guy
Though sometimes tempers flew;
He traded Jake his birthright
For a bowl of good hot stew.

Then Isaac, ill and blind,
Afraid that he would die,
Wanted to see Esau,
Firstborn blessings to apply.

But Jake was sure to grab
All that he could get.
And, pretending he was Esau,
He gambled and won the bet.

Esau went to raging
And vowed to get revenge.
He threatened to kill Jacob,
His birthright to avenge.

So Jacob made some fast tracks
To split that scene at once
And headed for his relatives—
A liar but not a dunce.

On the way, he had a vision
Of angels on a ladder.
God said, "I will give you
Blessings now and hereafter."

He met Rachel at a well.
It was love at first sight.
He worked for seven years
To marry and unite.

But he was tricked this time.
Getting sister Leah instead,
So he worked another seven
Then got Rachel to wed.

Traveling on the road,
He encountered a heavenly being.
They wrestled with each other.
Neither could win--it was grueling.

Oh, my goodness!
What a match took place
On the ground that very night.
It was a very close race.

They rolled all around,
All over each other.
Like children they were,
Not God and brother.

The Being said, "Let me go."
Jacob grabbed and said, "No way,
I've got you 'til you bless me.
Bless me this very day."

Then God grabbed hold of Jacob
Who listened to God's will
And waited on His orders,
His purpose to fulfill.

Jake, whose name became Israel,
For he had struggled with God,
Became father of the twelve tribes.
God had given him a nod.

Storm Clouds

Lake Arrowhead, Waleska, Georgia

# Job

## c. 2000-1800 B.C.

## Book of Job

Job lived in the land of Uz, which was probably located north of Palestine. He was a wealthy, married landowner, with ten children. He had prestige and possessions and was a happy, successful man.

One day, God was talking to Satan about what an upright man Job was. Satan claimed that Job was faithful only because he had wealth and good fortune. So God allowed Satan to test Job by taking almost everything away from him, even his health. Job and his friends believed that suffering came as a result of sin, but Job did not know what sin he had committed. Even Job's wife told him to "curse God and die."

Finally, God spoke to Job but never explained the reason for his suffering. All Job's riches were restored and more children were born. Through it all, Job never lost faith or blamed God.

Job is truly a riches-to-rags-to-riches story. It is one of the greatest stories of overcoming adversity in human history.

# *Job*

Job was a good man,
No doubt about that.
Lived a life of perfection
Until he fell flat.

He had it all,
A neighborhood star.
Was a living example,
Had come so far.

Seven sons and three daughters,
All kinds of wealth,
He continually thanked God
For his good health.

Satan approached God
And said with a smirk,
"I'll bet Job wouldn't last
If his life went berserk."

God said to test him
But to spare Job's life,
So Satan began
His siege of strife.

He killed all Job's children,
Took away his wealth.
He gave Job boils
And ruined his health.

Still Job was steadfast;
He wouldn't deny God.
His friends said he'd sinned,
His life was a fraud.

His wife suggested he
"Curse God and die,"
But all Job did
Was question God, "Why?"

God said, "I don't need your approval
For all that I do.
I created the universe,
Your friends, and you, too.

"Because you've been faithful,
I'll restore all you lost,
Your wealth, and your children.
You passed the test at great cost."

Satan lost his bet—
Job didn't cave.
He praised God always
From his birth to his grave.

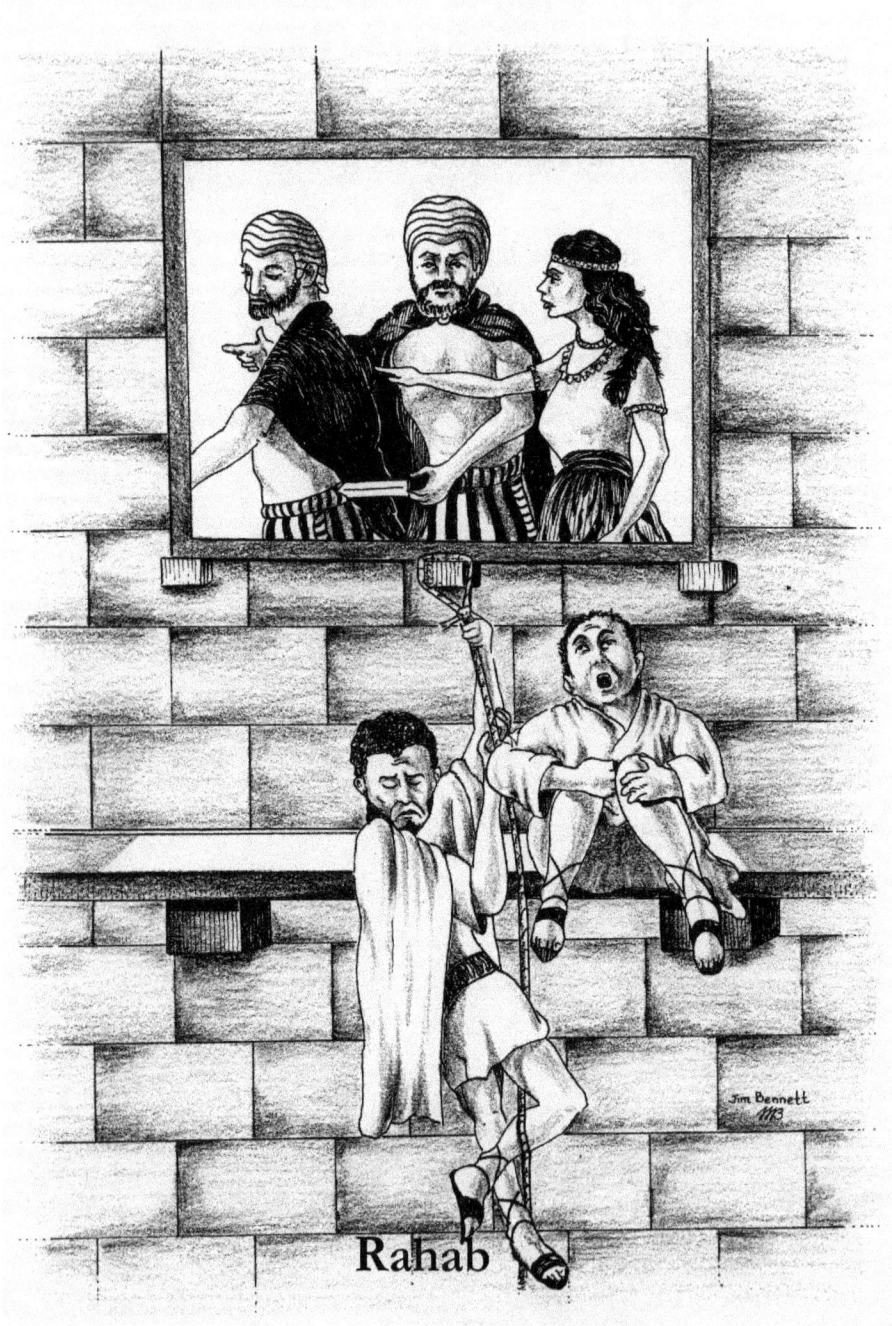

# *Rahab*

## *c. 1200 B.C.*
## *Joshua 2:1-16*

God told Joshua to conquer Jericho, so Joshua sent two spies into the city to study the situation. They went to see Rahab, a local prostitute who lived in a house in the city wall. Rahab had heard stories of the powers of the Israelite's God and believed them. She lied to the authorities and steered the soldiers in the wrong direction so the spies could escape. In return, she asked that she and her family be spared when the Israelites overran the city.

As God had promised, the Israelites did conquer the land, and Rahab and her family were spared.

## *Rahab*

Rahab lived in Jericho.
She made her living there,
Entertaining men of means--
Jericho didn't care.

Rahab lived conveniently,
A home in the city wall.
She knew sin and hard living
But was about to hear God's call.

Joshua sent two spies
To get all the information
From the city of Jericho
To aid in the invasion.

So the spies went to Rahab
For she knew all the news.
The Lord surely spoke to her;
She was about to pay her dues.

Since the King was already onto her,
He sent his soldiers to search.
But Rahab misguided them
And left them in the lurch.

The spies escaped
And gave Joshua the word
That to take all of the land
Was certainly not absurd.

So the priests led the way,
Holding the Covenant up high
Across the dry River Jordan—
Victory was nigh.

Seven days they circled the city,
Then the trumpet loudly blew;
The walls came tumbling down--
God and His Word were true.

Only Rahab escaped
Along with her family, too.
The Israelites won the day
And Canaan was theirs anew.

# David

# David

## c. 1100 B.C
## I Samuel

David was a shepherd boy who showed his bravery in facing the giant, Goliath, and defeating him with a slingshot. David ultimately became king, the greatest king of Israel, reigning over Judah and then over the United Kingdom of Israel. He was also known as a writer of psalms, a statesman, a soldier, a sage, and an ancestor of Jesus.

Alongside this list of his great qualities is another list--of David's many weaknesses and failures. He committed adultery with Bathsheba, after which he arranged the death of her husband. He disobeyed God on several occasions.

But despite all his sins, he loved God and passionately believed in God's faithful and forgiving nature. David was quick to confess his sins; his repentance was genuine, and he never took his own sins or God's forgiveness lightly.

He became known as a man after God's own heart.

## *David*

David was a splendid king,
All that Israel hope for.
He was an answer to their prayer
As the crown he proudly wore.

A shepherd boy was he,
Born of humble means;
He rose to fame and fortune
Under God's favor, it seems.

David was a psalmist,
His emotions ever nigh.
His songs were full of praise
For his God most high.

Samuel anointed David king
Much to Saul's distress,
And when David killed Goliath,
Saul felt more duress.

Saul was sorely jealous.
He aimed to take the life
Of David and his loyal men.
So began the strife.

But David won the day
And legally was the king
First of Judah, then all Israel--
Prosperity he would bring.

But, alas, he fell from grace
When Bathsheba he saw.
He took her, killed her husband--
Was he above God's law?

Prophet Nathan pointed out
The error of his way,
Of David's sin and guilt;
Now his family had to pay.

His son Absalom rebelled
But lost the battle true.
David mourned his son
And was very sad and blue.

David planned a temple
To truly honor God,
But didn't get to built it--
Shady paths he'd trod.

But God so loved David
He established his house forever.
Of him, Christ would descend
To be our Lord and Savior.

**Sheaf of Wheat
Western Nebraska**

# *Solomon*

## *c. 900 B.C.*
## *1 Samuel 12, I Kings 1-2, Chronicles 1*

Solomon was the son of David and Bathsheba. His major accomplishment was the building of the First Temple in Jerusalem. He was wise and wealthy and had immense power that finally corrupted him. But God loved Solomon and asked him what he wanted. Rather than asking for more riches or land, Solomon asked God for a discerning heart. God was so pleased with his answer that he granted Solomon's request and in addition gave him more riches.

In time, wanting his kingdom to grow, Solomon sealed a pact with Egypt by marrying the Pharaoh's daughter. She was the first of hundreds he married or took as concubines for political reasons, moves which were against

God's commands. Solomon went even further and built altars to the gods of the foreign wives.

He had disobeyed God and thereby lost half his kingdom. Solomon became disillusioned, feeling his life had been meaningless because he had turned away from God.

## *Solomon*

Solomon was a rich man.
He had lots of gold.
His wealth could not be measured,
His influence untold.

He was the son of David
And Bathsheba, too,
And highly favored in the land
For his wisdom true.

He had asked God for discernment
Instead of riches and gold,
Not the death of his enemies,
But to become wise and bold.

God was so pleased
At Solomon's request and choice
That he also gave him wealth,
Another reason to rejoice.

So Solomon built the temple,
A grand, elaborate place.
He covered it with gold,
And Lebanon cedars to brace.

Seven years later,
The temple was finally done.
His palace was in the making—
Solomon was having fun.

Yet he wasn't ever satisfied
Even with all his loot.
He married 700 women,
With 300 concubines to boot.

The women were to cement
His foreign relations abroad,
And to please each one's gods,
He built alters wherever they trod.

The Lord became angry;
He pronounced this decree:
The kingdom will be divided
And only Judah will be free.

So Solomon died a broken man;
For all his sins, he did pay.
Gold & wisdom couldn't save him
For he disobeyed God that day.

# *Elijah*

## *c. 800 B.C.*
## *I Kings*

Elijah was the greatest of the Hebrew prophets living in the ninth century B.C. He was a colorful, exciting character bringing down fire and brimstone from the skies, raising the dead, and ascending into heaven in a whirlwind. Elijah confronted Ahab regarding the king's allowing Baal priests and worshipers in the Temple.

The land had suffered from three years of drought. Elijah challenged the prophets of Baal to a contest between them and the God of Israel. The Baal prophets raved all afternoon but to no avail. Their god was silent. Elijah then called on the God of Israel to fill the water jars and rain down fire to burn the sacrifice. Thus, it was done.

King Ahab told Queen Jezebel what Elijah had done, and she was furious, saying she would have the prophet killed. Elijah escaped, feeling frustrated and afraid until God revealed Himself again in a tiny whisper.

## *Elijah Was a Prophet, Yeah!*

Elijah was a prophet, yeah!
He bugged the king all day.
He told him what he didn't want to hear;
God said the king must pay.

Elijah performed miracles, yeah!
God spoke through him aloud.
He stopped the rain, filled the jar;
He made God very proud.

Elijah was a hunted man, yeah!
The king looked all over.
If he had found him, he would kill him--
With great glee, moreover.

Elijah was a fearless man, yeah!
He called the king to him;
He challenged the prophets of Baal
To a dual of fire and brim.

Elijah was God's man, yeah!
He won the duel hands down
When the other prophets couldn't put forth
With either a smile or a frown.

Elijah chased the daylight, yeah!
He put Baal to shame;
He taunted and teased the prophets
And said they were to blame.

Elijah was a prophet, yeah!
He called upon the Lord.
The Lord won the day for him
With His fire and sword.

**Titmouse and Angel**

**Waleska, Georgia**

# Jeremiah-The Weeping Prophet

## c. 627-586 B.C.
## Book of Jeremiah

Jeremiah ministered under Judah's last five kings. He was a study in endurance as he delivered God's message to the people of Judah for forty years. His message was to repent and come away from their sins. He was ignored and ridiculed, his life threatened. He was thrown into prison and a cistern and taken to Egypt against his will. Jeremiah was persistent and passionate, but the people didn't listen. He depended on God alone for his strength and support as he declared his messages of doom, all the while weeping over the fate of his beloved country.

His prediction of Jerusalem's destruction came to pass as the Babylonians captured and destroyed the city and its temple in 586 B.C. The people were carried into exile to Babylon.

## *Jeremiah-The Weeping Prophet*

Jeremiah was especially called,
A message from God to bring.
He was ignored & harassed
By king after king after king.

He boldly warned the kings
Of God's judgment on sin,
To avoid idols & incense
Or the sorrows would begin.

But they never listened;
They thought they knew best.
They did their own thing
And stoned him like the rest.

But Jeremiah was faithful;
He depended on God's love.
Because his life was threatened,
His strength came from above.

He was also angry and sad
As he watched his fellows leave.
The Babylonians conquered all;
Surely, Judah would now believe.

But God spoke to Jeremiah
And showed him a pot of clay.
"I will remold this very pot
And shape it as I may.

"So will I reshape Israel;
I'm not done with them yet.
They will be a new nation;
They will multiply & beget.

"I will free them once again.
The new covenant will appear.
They will be my people.
I will always hold them dear.

"They will be returned
From their exile afar.
The holy city will be rebuilt;
Israel is still my shining Star."

## Roman Coliseum
## Rome, Italy

# *Daniel*

## *c. 627-586 B.C.*
## *Book of Daniel*

Daniel was another Jewish captive exiled to Babylon. Because of his ability to interpret the king's dreams, he was given a prominent position in the Babylonian government. He was advisor to two Babylonian kings and two Medo-Persian kings.

His three friends, Shadrach, Meshach, and Abednego, were also given positions in the government. The three refused to bow down to a golden image and were condemned to death in a fiery furnace, but God stepped in and spared their lives in the furnace.

David also remained faithful to God and was condemned to die in a den of lions. Again, God intervened, shut the mouths of the lions, and rescued Daniel. Daniel is known for his apocalyptic visions and gift of prophesy, which foretell God's plans for the future, including the coming of the Messiah. His visions were a sign of hope that God was in control of history and the people were to remain faithful.

# *Daniel*

Daniel in the lions' den,
A story every child knows.
Daniel held his convictions
As those hungry lions arose.

Oh, but God was in charge,
Not the lions or the king.
An angel tamed the lions;
Out of the den, Daniel came.

Daniel was in exile
In Babylon with the others,
But his gift of prophecy
Put him above his brothers.

He advised and prophesied
To four different kings,
But remained a man of prayer
Not swayed by other things.

His friends were also true
As they faced the fiery furnace
And walked out without a burn.
God saved them on purpose.

God remains in control,
No matter where we are—
In a den, in a furnace
Or held in lands afar.

# Ezekiel

## c. 593-571 B.C.
## Book of Ezekiel

Ezekiel was a priest who became a prophet delivering God's message to His people in exile in Babylon. God spoke directly to Ezekiel, telling him that Jerusalem would not escape destruction. God gave him many vivid visions of strange creatures, and Ezekiel became a powerful messenger.

A central theme of his message was the personal responsibility of each person to be accountable to God. God expected personal obedience and worship from each individual even in captivity. Ezekiel also had the difficult task of dispelling the false hope that Israel's captivity would be short, but he also brought a message of future hope. The vision of new life and a nation restored came in the form of the famous Valley of Dry Bones that represented the Jews in captivity--scattered and spiritually dead. The bones coming together again represented God's restoring life to spiritually dead people.

## *Ezekiel*

When Ezekiel encountered God,
He would never be the same.
God called him to bring a message,
Or Ezekiel would be to blame.

God wished him to be a prophet,
So in Babylon, his message did bring
After visions of four creatures
Each with four sides and wings.

God had poor Ezekiel
Do many strange things:
Like, lie on his side for awhile;
Eat only what God did bring.

He could speak only
When he had messages to bring.
God was planning Divine Surgery;
A new heart would be the thing.

They couldn't blame their fathers
For sins already past;
Each person was responsible
For sins that each had cast.

Ezekiel had many visions
Of chariots and forms of fire.
God appeared to him one day
With flame as his attire.

Ezekiel saw them dry bones.
They rattled all around;
They got up and got dressed
Right off that ol' bare ground.

Israel was those bones,
Brought back to life again.
God was with them in exile
Until their new nation began.

**Columns
Pompeii, Itlay**

# Haggai

## c. 500s B.C.
## Book of Haggai

In 586 B.C., the temple in Jerusalem was destroyed by the Babylonians. King Cyrus of Babylon permitted the Jews to return to their homeland in 538 B.C. to rebuild Jerusalem and their temple. At first, the people were diligent but then lost interest and gave in to the opposition, and the work was stopped.

Along with Zechariah, Haggai admonished the people about their poor values and indifference. The people listened and once again began restoring the temple. It was completed in 516 B.C.

## *Haggai*

The Jewish temple was destroyed
When the Babylonians swept it clean.
The Israelites tried hard to rebuild;
The opposition was really mean.

So the building was let go,
The progress set aside.
People became more interested
In their own lives outside.

Then once again, a prophet rose
To set their priorities straight.
Haggai, a man of God, spoke,
Saying, "Make the temple great.

"Get busy and finish the temple;
Get back on track again.
Bring on the cedar and the gold;
Let the building again begin."

He wandered in the streets,
Preaching from his heart:
"Set your priorities straight,
Get on your feet, and start."

Haggai urged the people
To get back to God's will,
And the temple was completed.
God said, "Haggai filled the bill."

# Esther

# *Esther*

## *c. 450 B.C.*

## *Book of Esther*

Drama, power, romance, and intrigue are all found in the story of Esther, a great woman and queen indeed. God made the plans and picked the characters, but they had to agree with God's wishes and plans, which they did. The Persian King Xerxes was married to Queen Vashti. During a drunken party, he ordered Vashti to appear before all his male friends. She refused and was sent away.

In the time that followed, Xerxes picked another beautiful young woman to be queen. Attendants took a year to get her ready. What Xerxes didn't know was that Esther was Jewish, and that Mordecai, a government official, was her relative.

A deceitful man, Haman was second in command to Xerxes, but Mordecai would not bow down to him. Haman determined to destroy Mordecai and all the Jews, so he fooled Xerxes into signing an edict condemning all the Jews to death. Mordecai convinced Esther to save her people, telling her, "Who knows? You may have been born for such a time as this." Esther came up with a brilliant scheme that resulted in Haman's being put to death instead of Mordecai. Her plan also saved the Jews, and she became a heroine among her people.

## *Esther--For Such A Time As This*

Vashti, Vashti,
What grit she had
To say no to King Xerxes,
Who could be mean and bad.

But she paid the price.
The king was "burning mad."
He had to save face,
So he threw her out, the cad.

Now he had to find
Another queen to reign,
So they rounded up the virgins
To choose one young and tame.

Wow! Esther was a looker;
Fair and lovely was she.
She caught Xerxes eye,
Soon his new queen to be.

She spent a year getting ready
With every beauty aid:
New clothes, makeup and the works
So her beauty would not fade.

Now Esther was a Jew,
But Xerxes didn't know.
"Don't tell," said Mordecai
"Just go with the flow."

Everything was dandy
For the first five years.
Then Haman stepped in,
And increased all the Jews' fears.

He was mad at Mordecai
For not bowing down,
So he told Xerxes
Jews threatened the crown.

So an edict was issued
To kill all the Jews,
And Mordecai appealed to Esther,
"If you snooze, you lose."

He told her, "Who knows?
Don't be amiss.
You may have been born
For such a time as this."

So Esther finally agreed
After all the prayer and fasting;
And she appeared before Xerxes--
Would her head be lasting?

But he handed her the scepter,
Which meant she saved her head,
And he granted her a wish
That Haman would come to dread.

Haman built a gallows
To hang Mordecai up high,
And went to Esther's banquet,
Not realizing it was his own good-bye.

Now Xerxes was all set
To repay Mordecai for a good deed.
So the king asked Haman
How to honor a man indeed.

*Well*, Haman thought, *of course*,
*There's no one else but me.*
So he named such fine things
As the King's robe and horse, you see.

He couldn't believe it
When Mordecai was named.
It was a sudden turn of events
Where Mordecai was honored, not blamed.

So, much to his chagrin,
Haman obeyed the King
And led Mordecai around
While his little song he did sing.

Now the King had promised Esther
Whatever she desired.
She quickly exposed Haman;
Her very best shot she fired.

Haman, terrified beyond measure,
Made a desperate move to be spared,
Threw himself on Esther's couch,
Assuming that she cared.

At that moment, the king returned.
He quickly surveyed the scene.
He saw Haman near his wife
And jealous, turned perfectly green.

The king was shocked; he was mad,
Mad as he could be,
And ordered Haman hanged
On that seventy-five-foot tree.

But still the Jews were in peril;
The edict was still in place.
But Esther was not done yet;
She was more than a pretty face.

Esther asked that her people live,
As she fell before the king.
Mordecai was given great honor
As well as the king's ring.

The Jews prevailed;
They survived the day.
God used His servants;
He had His say.

Oh, the mystery, the intrigue,
The irony of it all:
The one who struggled most to rise
Was the one who took the fall.

# The Written Word

# *Ezra*

## *c. 400 B.C.*
## *Book of Ezra*

Ezra was a priest, a scribe, and a great leader. His whole life was dedicated to serving God and God's people. He not only knew God's Word well, he believed and obeyed it.

About eighty years after the rebuilding of the temple, Ezra led the second group of exiles from Babylon to Jerusalem, returning with about 2,000 men and their families. His job was to teach others about God and how to live accordingly.

Upon returning to Jerusalem, he was appalled to discover how many there had married foreign women, disobeying God's command. He confronted the people with their sins. They heard him, confessed, and set out to rectify the situation. He and Nehemiah led the last spiritual awakening recorded in the Old Testament.

## *Ezra*

Ezra made his commitment
To study the Word of the Lord.
As an able scribe,
He could read and record.

He followed what he read
In the scriptures every day.
He obeyed and applied
Whatever they did say.

From there, he became a teacher,
Telling others how to apply
The Scriptures in their daily lives,
At least that they should try.

He came from Babylon
Back to the Holy City
And was shocked and disappointed--
What he found was a pity.

The Israelites had once again
Fallen short of God's plan.
They had married others
Outside of the Jewish clan.

Ezra was ashamed
Of all that his people had done.
He fell down in prayer
And summoned each leader and son.

He pointed out the sin
In taking a foreign wife,
And said they really were owed
More punishment and strife.

But he assured them, too,
Israel could be preserved,
And God would spare their nation
Far beyond what they deserved.

**Communion Cup**

**Smyrna, Georgia**

# *Nehemiah*

## *c. 400 B.C.*

## *Book of Nehemiah*

Nehemiah was a cupbearer for the Persian king, a great job. He, however, was greatly disturbed because the wall around Jerusalem had not been built even though the temple had been rebuilt seventy years earlier. He was a man of prayer, and God gave him a plan.

He left Persia and went to Jerusalem, praying all the while. He convinced the officials, the priests, and the nobles to rebuild the wall. He was a brilliant organizer and leader, and the wall was built in a record time of fifty-two days. He accomplished this even in the presence of great resistance.

Not only did he lead the people in rebuilding the wall, but he inspired a great spiritual reawakening.

# *Nehemiah*

When Nehemiah saw a problem,
He dove right in.
He didn't wait for someone else;
He stepped up to begin.

His life, comfy in Persia land,
Didn't matter to him a bit.
He went to Jerusalem where needed,
Knowing he was the right fit.

Nehemiah's first response
Was to ask God in prayer
For His direction and help
And for His loving care.

In fifty-two days, he up and managed
To get those walls rebuilt.
Not everyone was happy;
Some interfered without guilt.

But the walls kept going up
To protect the holy city.
Once more, God had provided
For the faithful and the gritty.

Nehemiah didn't quit
When the walls were up.
He continued to organize and plan
To get rid of the corrupt.

Nehemiah the governor
Led the people there.
He organized a meeting
Where Ezra could preach and declare.

The people were inspired;
A religious revival began
Because Nehemiah, man of action.
Picked up the ball and ran.

**Angel Lights**
**Waleska, Georgia**

# *Gabriel*

## *Luke 1*

Gabriel is an angel of God who is mentioned by name in the Bible at least three times, always bringing an important message from God. He appears to the prophet Daniel about 500 years before Christ and interprets Daniel's visions. In the New Testament, he appears to Zechariah in the temple, announcing to him that he and Elizabeth will have a child. God then sends Gabriel to visit Mary to tell her that she will bear the Son of God.

In both instances, Gabriel's first words were "Do not be afraid."

# *Gabriel*

Gabriel, blow your horn;
Blow it loud and clear;
Blow those sweet notes
For everyone to hear.

Gabriel, a special angel,
Brings only good news to earth.
You see, he works for God,
His messages of utmost worth.

Gabriel came to Zechariah
To inform him of a son.
He also came to Mary
To say she was the one.

They were both afraid,
Wouldn't we all be the same
If this heavenly being appeared
Dressed in light or in flame?

"Do not be afraid," he said,
"You have found favor with God."
That, in itself, was good news
Though to them it sounded quite odd.

He went on to say the message
God had given him to say,
And they both stood there in wonder
At the events of that special day.

Was it also Gabriel
Who said a babe was born
And told the lowly shepherds
In that very early morn?

Or did he appear to the Israelites
To lead them on their way?
Or come to roll the stone away
On Jesus' tomb that day?

We never know when he might appear
And bring good news to us;
Oh, what a thought that truly is.
I hope he looks like us.

# Zechariah

## Contemporary of Jesus
## Luke 1

Zechariah was the first to be told that Jesus was going to be born. He was a priest and was married to Elizabeth, a relative of Mary. For two weeks each year, Zechariah had to go to the temple in Jerusalem to perform his priestly duties. The year he was chosen to be the priest to enter the Holy Place of the temple and offer incense to God, Zechariah was surprised and afraid when the angel Gabriel appeared. His message from God was that he would have a son who would prepare the way for the Lord. Zechariah could hardly believe his ears and doubted that it could happen at their advanced ages.

Gabriel assured him that God would make it possible and that Zechariah would not be able to speak until their baby, John the Baptist, was born.

## *Zechariah*

When it came to duties
And doing them well,
Zechariah, the priest, did more
Then polish the bell.

He got up that morning
And marched to the temple,
For his turn had come
To light the candle.

Only once in his lifetime
Would he be allowed
To light the incense.
His best, he vowed.

He prayed for the people
Who waited outside,
But he added a prayer:
For a child, he cried.

Yes, he and wife Liz
Had been barren for years.
They were old now
And had cried all their tears.

His prayer went up
Like the incense smoke,
But God already knew
And then He spoke.

He sent Gabriel to tell him
They would have a child.
His name would be John
He'd look woolly and wild.

He'd be the one
To usher in the Lord,
To announce His coming.
Zechariah was floored.

How can that be,
In our old age?
Can we have a child
At this late stage?

The angel had had it;
Zechariah would be mute
Until the babe was born
In his birthday suit.

How to tell Liz
That she'd be with child,
As the angel declared.
Zech must have smiled.

The months went by—
At last Zech could acclaim,
The babe was really born
And John was his name.

**Madonna and Child**

Pantheon, Rome, Italy

## *Mary, Mother of Jesus*

### *Contemporary of Jesus*
### *Matthew 1:18; Luke 1, 2; John 2, 19*

Mary was a young lady living in Nazareth who was preparing to marry Joseph, a carpenter and descendent of David. She couldn't have guessed that God had special plans for her. One day, the angel Gabriel appeared to her and told her she would be the mother of the Son of God. She was still a virgin and wondered how that could be. Gabriel then told her that the baby would be God's son.

Mary's response was "I am the Lord's servant. May it be to me as you have said." She had the painful privilege of motherhood to Jesus. She was the only person who was present at both Jesus' birth and His death, when she watched Him die on the cross. While Jesus was on the cross, He asked the disciple John to care for His mother, Mary.

## *Mary, the Teen*

Mary was just a young thing,
An early teen, a young maid.
She was betrothed to Joseph,
A local carpenter by trade.

All set, she safely thought
To live a normal life,
To marry and have children,
Living as Joseph's wife.

Little did she know
Her destiny to become
The Mother of the Lord,
God's one and only son.

Gabriel appeared one day.
Mary was stunned and awed.
"Do not be afraid," he said.
"You have found favor with God.

"You will be with child
And give birth to a son,
The son of God, no less.
You are to be the one."

"Well, excuse me," she said
"I am still a virgin.
You must have the wrong girl,
But I am willing to listen."

"You have been chosen;
No, there's no mistake.
God will be with you
For your burden will be great."

With a tear in her eye,
Mary bowed her head.
"I am God's servant;
May it be as He said."

Now how do you suppose
She told Joseph the news,
Fearing that he would leave her
For he had a good excuse?

Joseph started to divorce her,
Very quietly, of course.
When an angel came to him
And said God was the source.

Mary ran to share the news
With Elizabeth, much her senior,
But she didn't have to tell her--
Elizabeth's baby stirred within her.

Elizabeth knew at once
That Mary carried the Lord,
And they both cried with joy
As their spirits happily soared.

They spent many happy days
Talking about their babies,
Talking about the little things,
The mysteries, miracles and maybes.

Then the time came
For Mary to return home,
And she went back to join Joseph
In their life together, Shalom.

## Sister Angels Tree Carving
### Galveston, Texas

# *Elizabeth*

## *Contemporary of Jesus*

## *Luke 1*

Elizabeth was married to Zechariah, a priest. They were "upright in the sight of God" for they not only outwardly complied with all the Jewish laws but obeyed the spirit of the law. Their greatest sorrow was that they had never been able to have any children. In Jewish culture, this was considered to be not having God's blessing. Now they were old and had given up hope of ever having a child.

That is, until Zechariah was visited in the temple by the angel Gabriel who said they were to be blessed with a child. The child was to be called John, and he would herald the coming of Jesus. However, because he had doubted God, Zechariah was made speechless until the birth of the baby, so he had a difficult time explaining the news to his wife. But Elizabeth was ecstatic with joy.

Elizabeth was a relative of Mary's, who also had a visit from Gabriel telling her that she would have a child--not just any child but the Son of God. Mary went immediately, traveled the seventy miles to visit Elizabeth, and spent time there as they shared their blessings and the coming births of their sons—Jesus and John, the Baptist!

## *Elizabeth and Mary*

Elizabeth was a Godly woman;
She followed all the rules God sent,
Not only what they said
But also what they meant.

Her faithfulness God noted
And He rid her of pain and shame;
He answered her longtime prayers:
Into her womb, a child came.

She had been old and baron,
Not able to bare a child.
So this child within her womb
Was her long-awaited God-Child.

But God blessed her further
And gave her the sight to see
That Mary was also with child
As she carried the Savior to be.

So Mary and Elizabeth
Helped each other to know
That God was using them
To help His people to grow.

Elizabeth soon gave birth to John
Who heralded our Lord's way.
Then Mary gave birth to Jesus--
God rejoiced on that birthday!

What a bond they had,
Watching their sons as they grew.
The boys seemed like any other,
But, oh, the Mothers knew.

**Dove at the Hermitage
Assisi, Italy**

# *Simeon and Anna*

## *Contemporaries of Jesus*

## Luke 2

As was the custom, Mary and Joseph took Jesus to the temple in Jerusalem to be consecrated when He was a month old. They went to make a sacrifice to God.

There was an old man named Simeon at the temple who recognized Jesus right away as the one he had been awaiting. It had been revealed to him earlier by the Holy Spirit that he would not die until he had seen the Lord's Christ, so he went to the temple to wait. He took Jesus in his arms and told the parents what God planned for their child and warned Mary of her future grief. Having seen the Messiah, Simeon could now die in peace.

At the temple that day, Anna was also awaiting the arrival of the Messiah. She was an old prophetess, meaning that she was close to God. She never left the temple and worshiped night and day, praying and fasting. She immediately recognized Jesus and gave thanks to God, identifying Jesus as the long-awaited Redeemer.

## *Simeon and Anna*

They had watched for years;
They had waited and waited
For the Messiah to come,
As God had stated.

God had promised
That Simeon would live
'Til he saw the Savior.
What more could He give?

So Simeon was faithful,
His eyes on the door;
As he grew old,
His eyesight grew poor.

But he had no trouble seeing
As Mary and Joseph came in.
He knew Jesus was the One,
God's mission to begin.

He took Jesus in his arms
And praised God out loud.
Now he could die in peace
As long ago he vowed.

As old as Methuselah--
Well, almost, it seems--
Was Anna the prophetess
With her hopes and dreams.

She lived at the temple,
Widowed years ago.
She, too, recognized Jesus.
Just how did she know?

God had said they'd know,
And they believed the Word.
So they watched and waited—
The event occurred.

# Simon Peter

## Contemporary of Jesus
## Matthew; Mark; Luke; John; Acts; Peter 1, 2

Jesus' first two disciples were the fishermen Peter and his brother, Andrew. His first words to them were "Come, follow me." At once, they left everything and went with Jesus. That was typical of Peter. He was impulsive and brash and spoke without thinking. Yet Jesus saw something strong and permanent in him as He named him Peter, the Rock.

Peter became one of the inner group of three among Jesus's disciples and the first great minister of the gospel. He loved Jesus dearly and even walked on water to go to Jesus on the Sea of Galilee until his fear caused him to sink.

In the Garden of Gethsemane, he tried to protect Jesus as the soldiers came to arrest Him. Acting impulsively, he cut off the ear of the high priest's servant. After Jesus was arrested, Peter bravely followed them to the courtyard but then denied Him three times before the cock crowed at sunrise, just as Jesus had predicted.

One of Peter's weaknesses was his difficulty in accepting the Gentile Christians as equals. He had many disagreements with Paul about this concept. Yet Peter remains one of the most loved characters in the Bible.

## *Simon Peter*

Peter was one of those guys
You just have to love.
He was impulsive and emotional;
He was no gentle dove.

Peter was a fisherman
And thought he was there to stay,
But Jesus spotted him right off.
This big one never got away.

Peter often spoke without thinking,
Putting his foot in his mouth,
And then he stumbled over his tongue
As everything seemed to go south.

But Jesus chose him anyway
Despite his sin and guilt;
Simon became Peter, the Rock
On which Christ's church was built.

Andrew was Pete's brother,
He led him to the Master.
The pace of their lives increased
As it got deeper and faster.

He and his brothers had been fishing
All night without a catch
When Jesus said to try again;
He would surely get a batch.

So Peter did as Jesus said:
They lowered their nets once more,
And then they caught so many fish
They had to hurry for the shore.

Jesus then said, "Follow me,"
And Peter didn't wait.
Immediately, he left the boat
To embrace his brand new fate.

Peter tried to walk on water
When Jesus told him, "Come."
He looked away, became afraid.
He sank a little, and then some.

Peter truly loved Jesus;
His zeal was at a peak.
His spirit was certainly strong,
But his body, oh so weak.

He then denied Jesus,
And he heard the cock's loud crow;
He hated all his words
And knew that Jesus would know.

Although he was still Peter,
He grew in wisdom and faith,
Still full of weaknesses, 'tis true
But saved by the Master's grace.

## 908 A.D. Olive Tree
### Pont de Gard, France

# Zaccheaus

## Contemporary of Jesus
## Luke 19:1-9

When Jesus was passing through Jericho, He came to a sycamore-fig tree and saw a man up in the tree. Because he was short of stature, Zacchaeus had climbed into the tree so he could see Jesus over the heads of the crowd.

Zacchaeus was a hated tax collector and a crooked one at that. Being a Jew, he had gone to work for the Romans collecting taxes, making him doubly despicable among the Jewish people.

Jesus looked up and told Zacchaeus to come down, that he was going home with him that day. Everyone was shocked, including Zaccheaus, that Jesus would socialize with such a person. Zacchaeus was so touched by Jesus' acceptance that he immediately volunteered to give half his possessions to the poor and to repay anyone he had cheated at four times the amount.

With Zacchaeus, Jesus illustrated that "the Son of Man came to seek and to save what was lost."

## *Zacchaeus, the Little Man*

They said Zacchaeus was little;
A wee little man was he.
He wanted badly to see Jesus
So he climbed the Sycamore tree.

Certainly short, that is true,
But a big man in the town.
He was the chief tax collector;
His name was quite renown.

He had cheated many a man
To get to his position.
He was very proud of himself;
He had achieved his vision.

But then he lost his pride
Hearing that Jesus was near.
He got so excited
He lost all his fear.

His problem now was to find
A way to catch a view
Of this man called Jesus of Nazareth,
This increasingly famous Jew.

Zacchaeus must have been
A sorry sight to behold,
Climbing up the tree in his robe--
Or so the story is told.

He simply couldn't believe it
When Jesus was drawing near
And telling him to get down,
His message abundantly clear.

Jesus said He was coming
To Zaccheaus' house to eat.
So Zach jumped down from the tree;
His life was now complete.

He said, "I will surely give
Half my wealth to the poor
And repay all my debts.
Greed will rule me no more."

What shocking news this was
To the people of the town.
They just couldn't believe it;
Zacchaeus was so low down.

But Jesus was thrilled and pleased
That Zacchaeus had repented.
His new life had begun.
His old life was now ended.

Together, they rejoiced
As they walked along the way.
History was made
In Jericho that day.

Mary and Martha

# Mary and Martha

## Contemporaries of Jesus
## Matthew, Mark, Luke, and John

Mary and her older sister, Martha, lived in Bethany and were good friends with Jesus. He often stayed in their home when He was in that area.

Hospitality was a social requirement in the Jewish culture, and Martha was good at it. She was concerned with the details and the comfort of her guests; she was in control. Mary, on the other hand, was more interested in being with their guests, talking, and listening. When Jesus was visiting, Martha became distraught that Mary was not helping, and she complained.

Jesus gently corrected her attitude and told her that although her priorities were good, they were not the best. Again, Martha became upset and questioned Jesus when her brother, Lazarus, died. She questioned Jesus' power over death. And again, Jesus calmed her fears and doubts, raising Lazarus from the dead.

## *Mary and Martha*

Mary and Martha
were quite a pair:
Sisters of contrast,
All would declare.

Martha took charge;
She knew what to do;
She made a long list
Of things to review.

Now Mary was different;
She daydreamed a lot;
She loved people more
Than the things that she got.

Martha asked Jesus
To luncheon that day.
She was glad to see Him
For He'd been away.

"Martha," said Jesus,
"Come sit at my feet.
Come out of the kitchen,
My words are your treat."

Martha was busy—
So busy was she,
Preparing their lunch,
Of course, doing duty.

"What about Mary?"
She asked, perturbed.
"Why isn't she helping?
I'm very disturbed!"

"Mary has chosen
To be by my side,
To hear my words,
In my presence abide.

"I know you mean well
But your priorities lack.
You tend to confuse,
Nitpick, and sidetrack.

"Don't mix up the good
For the best, my dear.
Come, be with Me
Listen, and hear."

## Portrait of a Tree
## Waleska, Georgia

# Judas Iscariot

## Contemporary of Jesus
## The Gospels and Acts

We will never in this life know Judas' motive for betraying Jesus in the Garden of Gethsemane. We do know that he was sorry and tried to undo the evil by returning to the priests the money they had paid him.

Judas Iscariot was the only non-Galilean chosen by Jesus to be one of the disciples. He was also chosen to be the treasurer for the group and to keep the money bag. He was untrustworthy and stole money for himself from their funds.

He also approached the chief priests about having Jesus arrested, a plan for which he was paid thirty pieces of silver. He led a mob of people to arrest Him and identified Jesus with a kiss.

**When Judas saw that Jesus was going to be killed, he was "seized with remorse" and tried to appeal to the chief priests. They just laughed at him, so he threw down the money and went away and hanged himself.**

## *Judas Iscariot–Quite a Study*

Now, Judas, there you go—
A study in human behavior.
Exactly what did he believe
About Jesus, the Savior?

Did he think Jesus was really
The King of the Jews for sure?
Was he trying to force Jesus' hand,
Or was he still unsure?

Or maybe he didn't believe Him
And was greedy beyond belief;
Wanting thirty pieces of silver
Made him no better than a thief.

Jesus chose Judas to be a disciple,
Letting him keep the money bag.
Was Judas born to be evil,
Or did he change to a scallywag?

Judas signed a pact with the devil
To get Jesus arrested at dark.
He led the soldiers and kissed Him,
Which gave the soldiers their mark.

Judas was successful;
The soldiers took Jesus away.
Our Lord ended up before Pilate
To be crucified that day.

Judas realized his mistake,
And he tried to make amends.
But it was too late, the damage done.
Despairing, his life he'd end.

## Tree at Manassas Battlefield
## Virginia

# *Barabbas*

## *Contemporary of Jesus*
## *Matthew 27:21-2, John 18:40*

Barabbas had led an insurrection against the Roman government and had killed Roman citizens. He was being held, awaiting his execution, when Jesus was arrested and brought to Pilate because the Jewish high priests had no authority to execute anyone. Pilate found no fault with Jesus and tried to release Him. He gave the people a choice of whom to release— Jesus or Barabbas.

Some of the people considered Barabbas a hero because he had stood up against Rome. The high priests had also convinced the crowd to call for Barabbas' release. When Pilate ask what should be done with Jesus, they shouted, "Crucify Him, crucify Him."

So Jesus died in Barabbas' place and Barabbas was set free.

## *Barabbas*

Barabbas was quite a man;
Mean as a snake, they say.
Murdered and robbed with no regret,
Thinking the Romans should pay.

He gathered a mob, led a revolt
Against the oppressing forces.
Violence was the answer, he thought;
Hate and weapons were his sources.

So he was arrested, thrown into prison
To be crucified, he knew.
Still he scorned the ruling powers;
To his nature, he was true.

But he awoke one early morn
To a big surprise in the yard.
The guards brought him to Pilate,
Who played him like a trump card.

Pilate thought that the Jewish crowd
Would choose Barabbas to die,
But instead they chose Jesus.
"Crucify Him,"-- the cry.

What a stroke of luck he had that day
As he strutted off the stage.
Pilate just washed his hands of it
As the crowd continued to rage.

They had chosen the way of violence,
Of killing and of force,
Instead of the peaceful solution and love,
Which Jesus did endorse.

## Twin Roads
## Lake Arrowhead, Waleska, Georgia

# *Paul, Da' Man*

## *Paul's Ministry: 35-67 A.D.*
## *Acts, Paul's letters*

Paul was "da' man" who shaped the history of the Christian church more than anyone except Jesus. His name was Saul of Tarsus. He was a Jewish Pharisee and a Roman citizen, well trained and educated in the religious writings, as well as a tentmaker by trade. He believed that Christianity was dangerous to Judaism and persecuted the Christians without mercy. He was even present at Stephen's stoning.

On his way to Damascus to round up Christians, he was blinded by a brilliant light and confronted by Jesus Himself. Paul was never the same. He became as passionate in his belief for Christianity as he had been against it. God had chosen him to carry Christ's name and teachings to the gentiles.

Paul made three missionary journeys across the Roman Empire and wrote letters to the various churches, some while he was in a Roman prison. These letters later became a part of the New Testament. Paul did not always agree with the other disciples. Among the thorny issues was whether Gentiles had to obey Jewish laws before they could become Christians. Paul had to work hard to convince both the Jews and the gentiles themselves that the gentiles were acceptable.

## *Paul Was "Da' Man"*

If anyone could switch
From being bad to good,
Then Paul would fit the bill.
He did because he could.

Of course, he had some help
Like a blinding light from heaven
And God's voice that said,
"Quit persecuting my brethren."

He was a loyal Pharisee
Who knew the scriptures well.
He hated all the Christians—
They were dangerous, he could tell.

He had set out to destroy them,
Watched Stephen being stoned.
He had no feeling or mercy,
For their sins must be atoned.

But, *bam*, what a jolt he had
When the Lord got hold of him.
He turned around in midstream,
Knowing he must sink or swim.

He became as passionate for Christ
As he had been on the other side
And set out to convert the world,
Traveling the empire wide.

He and Peter didn't always agree
About converting the Gentiles.
Neither was a man of restraint;
They lived different lifestyles.

Paul made many missionary journeys,
Traveling far and wide,
Was falsely accused, and imprisoned.
Many wrongs were implied.

He certainly was bold,
Stirring trouble with the Jews,
Who took him to the Romans
With treason the issue.

But Gallio would have none of it
And told them to be on their way.
God told Paul, "Don't be afraid;
Just keep on having your say."

So Paul went to writing letters
To the churches of his day,
To the Romans and Corinthians,
Bold in what he had to say.

Paul did, however, suffer
With a thorn in the flesh;
"When I am weak, I am strong."
God provided him strength afresh.

Paul continued for many years,
The former Saul of Tarsus,
Preaching the salvation of Christ
To all those lost and godless.

## Carving on Door
## Simpsonwood, Atlanta, Georgia

## *Jesus*

Jesus, Jesus, why did you leave?
Why did you go away?
Why did you hang on the cross?
To pay for our sins, you say?

It all began centuries before
When sin arrived on earth,
When God promised a Savior,
Born through Virgin Birth.

The prophets preached and pleaded;
They prophesied for years.
They told of the One to come,
To relieve us of our fears.

Yes, Jesus, the One and Only,
The Son of God came to earth,
Came a babe in the stable.
Mother Mary gave Him birth.

He played and ran like other boys,
Learned scripture He already knew,
Stunned the leaders at the temple.
In wisdom, He daily grew.

One day, He met his cousin, John,
Who baptized Him in the water.
A dove descended on his head;
God said, "There is no other."

Jesus chose a selected few
To be His disciples then,
To carry on His work and word,
To be His top twelve men.

He healed the lame,
Spoke to young and old,
And raised the dead
As the scriptures foretold.

The crowds grew
As He traveled around.
No home did He own,
Sleeping on the ground.

The religious leaders
Grew increasingly nervous,
Were afraid for their place
And also quite jealous.

They must do away
With this thorn in the side,
The one who threatened
Their status and pride.

So they beseeched Rome
To get rid of this man,
To crucify Him;
That was their plan.

Jesus was arrested,
Condemned to death.
Hanging on a cross,
He took His last breath.

Don't despair that it's Friday
And Christ's on the cross.
Sunday is soon coming,
God's win, the Devil's loss.

Jesus, Jesus, Our One and Only
You didn't go away.
Sunday came, and You arose
To be with us every day.

# *Acknowledgments*

Many thanks go to my family who listened patiently and tirelessly to each new poem. A special thanks goes to my son, Scott, for the suggestion of the title, *"A Nod to God."*.

I am deeply grateful to my illustrator, Jim Bennett, for sharing his amazing talent in creating the illustrations for some of the poems. I smile every time I look at them.

And deep gratitude goes to my friend, Joan McFather, who generously edited every poem with precision and her meticulous attention to detail. She made every poem even better. I always thought, *Now why didn't I think of that?*

And I appreciate all my friends who listened and encouraged me to write this book.

# ***Illustrations and Photographs***

Corra Harris Chapel Window
    Cherokee County, Georgia
    Photo by Carolyn Burkholder
Waleska United Methodist Church
    Waleska, Georgia
    Photo by Carolyn Burkholder
Majestic Oak at Sunrise
    Waleska, Georgia
    Photo by Carolyn Burkholder
Adam and Eve
    Illustration by Jim Bennett
Noah
    Illustration by Jim Bennett
Llama With Beautiful Eyes
    Waleska, Georgia
    Photo by Carolyn Burkholder
Storm Clouds
    Waleska, Georgia
    Photo by Carolyn Burkholder
Rahab
    Illustration by Jim Bennett
David
    Illustration by Jim Bennett
Sheaf of Wheat
    Western Nebraska
    Photo by Carolyn Burkholder

Elijah
    Illustration by Jim Bennett
Titmouse and Angel
    Waleska, Georgia
    Photo by Carolyn Burkholder
Roman Coliseum
    Rome, Italy
    Photo by Carolyn Burkholder
Ezekiel
    Illustration by Jim Bennett
Columns
    Pompeii, Italy
    Photo by Carolyn Burkholder

Esther
    Illustration by Jim Bennett
The Written Word
    Photo by Carolyn Burkholder
Communion Cup
    Photo by Carolyn Burkholder
Angel Lights
    Photo by Carolyn Burkholder
Zechariah
    Illustration by Jim Bennett
Madonna and Child
    Pantheon, Rome, Italy
    Photo by Carolyn Burkholder
Sister Angels Tree Carving
    Galveston, Texas
    Photo by Carolyn Burkholder
Dove at the Hermitage
    Assisi, Italy
    Photo by Carolyn Burkholder

Simon Peter
    Illustration by Jim Bennett
908 A.D. Olive Tree
    Pont de Gard, France
    Photo by Carolyn Burkholder
Mary and Martha
    Illustration by Jim Bennett
Portrait of a Tree
    Waleska, Georgia
    Photo by Carolyn Burkholder
Tree at Manassas Battlefield
    Virginia
    Photo by Carolyn Burkholder

Twin Roads
    Lake Arrowhead, Waleska, Georgia
    Photo by Carolyn Burkholder
Carving on Door
    Simpsonwood, Atlanta, Georgia
    Photo by Carolyn Burkholder

www.ingramcontent.com/pod-product-compliance
Lightning Source LLC
Chambersburg PA
CBHW061945070426
42450CB00007BA/1061